CONTENTS

Copyright
Epigraph
Preface
Chapter 1   1
The Significance of Marketing Strategy   2
Diving Deeper: The Components of Marketing Strategy   3
Practical Guidance for Small Business Owners   5
Conclusion   9
Chapter 2   10
Understanding the Importance of Market Research   11
Navigating the Waters of Consumer Behavior   12
Mapping Out the Competitive Landscape   13
Forecasting Trends and Anticipating Changes   15
Practical Guidance for Small Business Owners   16
Conclusion   20
Chapter 3   21
Understanding the Importance of Marketing Objectives   22
Plotting Your Course: The SMART Approach to Goal Setting   23
Practical Guidance for Small Business Owners   25
Conclusion   27
Chapter 4   28

Understanding the Significance of Your Unique Value Proposition	29
Crafting Your Unique Value Proposition: The Art and Science of Differentiation	30
Practical Guidance for Small Business Owners	32
Conclusion	34
Chapter 5	35
Understanding the Significance of Marketing Channels	36
Navigating the Seas of Marketing Channels: Exploring Your Options	37
Practical Guidance for Small Business Owners	39
Conclusion	41
Chapter 6	42
Understanding the Marketing Mix: A Recipe for Success	43
Crafting Your Marketing Mix: Blending Strategies for Success	45
Practical Guidance for Small Business Owners	47
Conclusion	49
Chapter 7	50
Understanding the Importance of a Marketing Plan	51
Crafting Your Marketing Plan: A Step-by-Step Guide	52
Practical Guidance for Small Business Owners	54
Conclusion	56
Chapter 8	57
Understanding the Importance of Implementation and Evaluation	58
Implementing Your Marketing Strategy: Putting Plans into Action	59
Evaluating Your Marketing Strategy: Measuring Impact and Effectiveness	61

Copyright © 2024 Chimezie Igwe

All rights reserved

The characters and events portrayed in this book are fictitious. Any similarity to real persons, living or dead, is coincidental and not intended by the author.

No part of this book may be reproduced, or stored in a retrieval system, or transmitted in any form or by any means, electronic, mechanical, photocopying, recording, or otherwise, without express written permission of the publisher.

ISBN: 9798324366414
Imprint: Independently published

Cover design by: Art Painter
Library of Congress Control Number: 2018675309
Printed in the United States of America

"In the vast ocean of entrepreneurship, the only limits are those we impose upon ourselves. With vision as our compass and determination as our anchor, we chart our course toward uncharted horizons, guided by the stars of innovation and fueled by the winds of possibility."

CHIMEZIE IGWE

Practical Guidance for Small Business Owners	63
Conclusion	65
Chapter 9	66
Understanding the Need for Adaptation	67
The Art of Adapting Your Strategy	68
Practical Guidance for Small Business Owners	70
Conclusion	72
Chapter 10	73
The Power of Case Studies and Best Practices	74
Uncovering Lessons from Real-Life Stories	75
Best Practice: Personalized Customer Experience	77
Best Practice: Niche Targeting and User Experience	79
Practical Guidance for Small Business Owners	80
Conclusion	82
Chapter 11	83
Reflecting on the Journey	84
Key Takeaways and Lessons Learned	85
Looking to the Future	87
Final Words of Encouragement	88

PREFACE

Setting Sail on the Entrepreneurial Voyage

Ahoy, fellow adventurers of the business world! Welcome aboard as we embark on a thrilling journey into the heart of entrepreneurship. In this preface, allow me to extend my warmest greetings and set the stage for the exhilarating voyage that lies ahead.

The Call of Entrepreneurship

For many of us, the call of entrepreneurship is a siren song that beckons us to explore uncharted waters, pursue our passions, and chart our own course toward success. It's a journey filled with excitement, adventure, and endless possibilities—a journey where every wave brings new challenges and every sunrise brings new opportunities.

As we stand on the cusp of this grand adventure, it's important to recognize the courage and conviction that brought us here. Whether you're a seasoned entrepreneur with years of experience under your belt or a wide-eyed dreamer setting sail on your maiden voyage, know that you possess the spirit of a true pioneer—a spirit that dares to dream, dares to innovate, and dares to defy the odds.

Navigating the Waters of Business Strategy and Marketing

In the pages that follow, we'll embark on a comprehensive exploration of the principles, strategies, and tactics that form the bedrock of successful entrepreneurship. From crafting a compelling vision and mission to defining your target audience, developing a marketing strategy, and navigating the complexities of the modern marketplace, we'll cover all aspects of the entrepreneurial journey with depth, clarity, and practicality.

Through a combination of theoretical insights, real-world case studies, and actionable best practices, we'll arm ourselves with the knowledge, skills, and strategies needed to navigate the turbulent seas of business with confidence and competence. Whether you're seeking to launch a startup, grow an existing business, or simply enhance your understanding of the entrepreneurial landscape, this guide is designed to be your trusted companion and compass on the voyage ahead.

A Note of Gratitude

Before we set sail, I'd like to extend my heartfelt gratitude to all those who have contributed to the creation of this guide. From the pioneering entrepreneurs whose stories inspire us to the tireless researchers and experts whose insights illuminate our path, this journey is a testament to the collective wisdom and spirit of innovation that defines the entrepreneurial community.

To my fellow adventurers, I offer my sincerest wishes for a safe and successful journey. May the winds of fortune be ever at your back, and may your entrepreneurial dreams take flight on the wings of possibility. Together, let us embark on this voyage with courage, curiosity, and camaraderie, knowing that the greatest adventures await those bold enough to seize them.

Fair winds and following seas, my friends. Let the journey begin!

CHAPTER 1
Introduction to Marketing Strategy: Navigating the Path to Success

Welcome to the exciting world of marketing strategy, where the seeds of business success are sown and nurtured. As a small business owner, you're no stranger to the exhilarating highs and challenging lows of entrepreneurship. In this chapter, we'll embark on a comprehensive exploration of marketing strategy, diving deep into its intricacies, unpacking its significance, and equipping you with the knowledge and tools you need to chart a course toward sustainable growth and prosperity.

THE SIGNIFICANCE OF MARKETING STRATEGY

Imagine your business as a ship setting sail on the vast ocean of the market. Without a clear destination or a well-defined route, you're at the mercy of unpredictable winds and shifting currents. This is where marketing strategy comes into play—it serves as your compass, guiding you toward your goals and steering you away from treacherous waters.

At its essence, marketing strategy is the art and science of positioning your business in the hearts and minds of your target audience. It encompasses a myriad of interconnected decisions and actions aimed at understanding, attracting, and retaining customers. Without a robust marketing strategy, your business risks drifting aimlessly, struggling to gain traction in a crowded market place and failing to capitalize on its full potential.

DIVING DEEPER: THE COMPONENTS OF MARKETING STRATEGY

Let's peel back the layers of the marketing strategy onion to uncover its core components, each playing a pivotal role in shaping the trajectory of your business.

1. **Market Research and Analysis**: Think of market research as your compass, guiding you toward profitable opportunities and away from potential pitfalls. By delving deep into the wants, needs, and preferences of your target audience, you gain invaluable insights that inform every aspect of your marketing strategy. From demographic data and psychographic profiles to competitor analysis and trend forecasting, market research lays the foundation for strategic decision-making.

2. **Setting Marketing Objectives**: Like a captain plotting a course, setting clear and measurable marketing objectives is essential for charting a path toward success. Whether your goal is to increase brand awareness, drive website traffic, or boost sales, your objectives should be specific, attainable, relevant, and time-bound (SMART). By anchoring your strategy in concrete goals, you provide a clear direction for your efforts and a yardstick for measuring progress.

3. **Crafting Your Unique Value Proposition (UVP)**: In a

sea of competitors vying for attention, your UVP is the beacon that guides weary sailors to your shores. It's the promise you make to your customers—the unique blend of features, benefits, and experiences that sets you apart from the competition. By articulating your UVP with clarity and conviction, you create a compelling reason for customers to choose you over alternatives, fostering loyalty and advocacy in the process.

4. **Selecting Marketing Channels**: With an abundance of marketing channels at your disposal—from traditional print media and television ads to digital platforms like social media and email marketing—choosing the right mix can feel overwhelming. The key is to align your channel selection with the preferences and behaviors of your target audience, ensuring your message reaches them where they are most receptive. By striking the right balance between reach, relevance, and return on investment, you maximize the impact of your marketing efforts.

5. **Developing Your Marketing Mix**: Your marketing mix is the canvas upon which you paint your brand's story, blending the four Ps—product, price, place, and promotion—to create a masterpiece that resonates with your audience. From refining your product offerings and pricing strategy to optimizing your distribution channels and promotional tactics, each element plays a crucial role in shaping customer perceptions and driving purchase decisions. By harmonizing these elements into a cohesive strategy, you create a symphony of value that delights customers and drives business results.

PRACTICAL GUIDANCE FOR SMALL BUSINESS OWNERS

Armed with a deeper understanding of the components of marketing strategy, let's explore some practical guidance to help you navigate the complexities of the marketing landscape with confidence and clarity.

1. **Start with Your Audience**: Your customers are the compass that guides your business toward success. Take the time to understand their needs, preferences, and pain points, using tools like surveys, interviews, and focus groups to uncover valuable insights. By putting yourself in their shoes, you gain a deeper understanding of what drives their behavior and how you can position your brand to meet their needs effectively.

2. **Set Clear Objectives**: Like a lighthouse on a stormy night, clear objectives provide a guiding light for your marketing efforts. Whether your goal is to increase brand awareness, drive lead generation, or boost sales, articulating your objectives with clarity and specificity provides a roadmap for success. By setting measurable milestones and timelines, you create a framework for accountability and progress tracking, empowering you to course-correct as needed along the way.

3. **Stay Flexible and Adaptive**: In the ever-evolving landscape of business, adaptability is the key to

survival. Keep your finger on the pulse of market trends, consumer behavior, and competitive dynamics, remaining nimble and responsive to change. Whether it's adjusting your messaging in response to shifting consumer preferences or pivoting your channel strategy to capitalize on emerging opportunities, agility is your greatest asset in navigating the winds of change.

4. **Measure Your Results**: Effective marketing is rooted in data, not guesswork. Leverage analytics tools to track the performance of your marketing campaigns, measuring key metrics such as website traffic, conversion rates, and customer acquisition costs. By analyzing this data in real-time, you gain actionable insights into what's working, what's not, and where you can optimize for greater impact. Whether it's A/B testing different ad creatives or refining your targeting criteria based on audience engagement, let data be your compass in guiding strategic decision-making.

5. **Stay True to Your Brand**: Your brand is more than just a logo or a tagline—it's the soul of your business, the essence of who you are and what you stand for. Stay true to your brand values and personality in everything you do, from the tone and style of your messaging to the design and aesthetics of your marketing collateral. By fostering authenticity and consistency across all touchpoints, you build trust and credibility with your audience, cultivating lasting relationships that transcend transactions.

6. **Embrace Digital Transformation**: In today's digital age, embracing technology is no longer a choice—it's a necessity for survival. Explore digital marketing avenues such as social media advertising, search engine optimization (SEO), and content marketing to expand your reach and engage with your target audience effectively. Invest in user-friendly website

design and mobile optimization to ensure seamless browsing experiences for your customers. Leverage customer relationship management (CRM) tools to manage and nurture your customer relationships, providing personalized experiences that drive loyalty and retention.

7. **Cultivate Brand Advocacy**: Your most valuable marketing asset isn't your budget or your ad spend—it's your loyal customers. Cultivate brand advocacy by exceeding customer expectations at every touchpoint, delivering exceptional products, services, and support that inspire rave reviews and referrals. Encourage satisfied customers to share their experiences on social media, review platforms, and word-of-mouth channels, amplifying your brand's reach and influence organically. Invest in building a community around your brand, fostering a sense of belonging and camaraderie that transforms customers into loyal advocates and ambassadors.

8. **Stay Agile in Execution**: In the fast-paced world of business, agility is the name of the game. Embrace an agile mindset in your marketing approach, iterating quickly and adapting to changing circumstances with speed and efficiency. Embrace lean methodologies such as rapid experimentation, test-and-learn cycles, and continuous improvement to optimize your marketing efforts iteratively. Break down silos between marketing, sales, and customer service teams, fostering cross-functional collaboration and alignment that accelerates decision-making and execution. By staying nimble and responsive to market dynamics, you position your business for success in an ever-changing landscape.

9. **Invest in Education and Development**: The world of marketing is vast and ever-evolving, with new technologies, trends, and strategies emerging at a rapid

pace. Invest in your own education and development, staying informed about the latest industry insights, best practices, and innovations. Attend workshops, webinars, and conferences to expand your knowledge and network with industry peers. Enroll in online courses and certifications to deepen your expertise in areas such as digital marketing, analytics, and consumer behavior. By investing in continuous learning and professional development, you equip yourself with the skills and insights needed to stay ahead of the curve and drive meaningful results for your business.

10. **Foster a Culture of Innovation**: Innovation is the lifeblood of business growth, driving creativity, differentiation, and competitive advantage. Foster a culture of innovation within your organization, empowering employees at all levels to contribute ideas, experiment with new approaches, and challenge the status quo. Create dedicated spaces and initiatives for brainstorming, ideation, and collaboration, providing resources and support for innovative projects to flourish. Celebrate and recognize successful innovations, whether they result in incremental improvements or transformative breakthroughs, fostering a culture of curiosity, risk-taking, and continuous improvement that fuels long-term success.

CONCLUSION

In this expanded chapter, we've delved deep into the intricacies of marketing strategy, exploring its significance, unpacking its components, and providing practical guidance for small business owners to navigate the complexities of the marketing landscape with confidence and clarity. By embracing the foundational principles of marketing strategy, adopting a customer-centric mindset, and leveraging the latest tools and techniques, you're poised to chart a course toward sustainable growth and prosperity in today's dynamic business environment. So set your sails high, embrace the journey ahead with enthusiasm and determination, and let the winds of opportunity carry you toward a brighter future for your business and beyond.

CHAPTER 2
Market Research and Analysis: Navigating the Sea of Customer Insights

Welcome aboard as we embark on a voyage into the realm of market research and analysis—the compass that guides your business toward the shores of success. In this chapter, we'll dive deep into the waters of consumer behavior, competitor landscapes, and trend forecasting, equipping you with the knowledge and tools you need to navigate the complexities of the market with confidence and clarity.

UNDERSTANDING THE IMPORTANCE OF MARKET RESEARCH

Picture your business as a ship sailing through uncharted waters. Without a map or a compass to guide you, you're at the mercy of unpredictable currents and hidden obstacles. Market research serves as your navigational aid, providing insights into the needs, preferences, and behaviors of your target audience. By understanding the lay of the land, you can chart a course that leads to profitable opportunities and avoids potential pitfalls.

At its core, market research is about asking the right questions and listening to the answers. It's about uncovering the motivations behind consumer decisions, identifying emerging trends and opportunities, and gaining a deeper understanding of your competitive landscape. Whether you're launching a new product, entering a new market, or seeking to better understand your customers, market research is the compass that points you in the right direction.

NAVIGATING THE WATERS OF CONSUMER BEHAVIOR

Understanding your customers is the cornerstone of effective market research. Just as a captain must know the seas they sail; you must know the consumers you serve. Who are they? What are their needs and desires? What factors influence their purchasing decisions? These are the questions that market research seeks to answer.

One of the most powerful tools in your market research arsenal is the customer persona—a detailed profile of your ideal customer. By creating personas based on demographic, psychographic, and behavioral data, you can gain valuable insights into your target audience's preferences, pain points, and purchasing behaviors. From there, you can tailor your marketing efforts to resonate with their needs and aspirations, increasing the likelihood of success.

Consumer behavior is influenced by a myriad of factors, including cultural norms, social influences, and psychological triggers. By delving into the underlying motivations and drivers of consumer behavior, you can uncover valuable insights that inform your marketing strategy. For example, understanding the principles of social proof and scarcity can help you create more persuasive messaging and offers that resonate with your audience's subconscious desires.

MAPPING OUT THE COMPETITIVE LANDSCAPE

Just as a sailor must be aware of other vessels on the water, you must be aware of your competitors in the market. Competitive analysis is an essential component of market research, providing insights into rival offerings, pricing strategies, and marketing tactics. By understanding the strengths and weaknesses of your competitors, you can identify gaps in the market and opportunities for differentiation.

SWOT analysis—examining the strengths, weaknesses, opportunities, and threats facing your business and its competitors—is a valuable tool for competitive analysis. By identifying your strengths and weaknesses, as well as those of your competitors, you can develop strategies to capitalize on your advantages and mitigate your vulnerabilities. Additionally, analyzing industry trends and market dynamics can help you anticipate shifts in consumer preferences and stay one step ahead of the competition.

Competitive analysis should go beyond surface-level observations to uncover deeper insights into your competitors' strategies and tactics. This may involve analyzing their marketing campaigns, studying their product offerings, and monitoring their online presence and customer reviews. By understanding what sets your competitors apart and how they position themselves in the market, you can identify opportunities to differentiate your own brand and capture market share.

FORECASTING TRENDS AND ANTICIPATING CHANGES

Just as a seasoned navigator reads the stars to predict the weather, you must read the signs in the market to anticipate trends and changes. Trend forecasting is an essential aspect of market research, helping you stay ahead of the curve and capitalize on emerging opportunities.

One way to forecast trends is by monitoring consumer behavior and sentiment through social listening and sentiment analysis. By analyzing online conversations, reviews, and social media mentions, you can identify emerging trends and topics of interest to your target audience. Additionally, staying informed about macroeconomic factors, technological advancements, and regulatory changes can help you anticipate shifts in the market landscape and adapt your strategy accordingly.

Trend forecasting is not just about predicting the future —it's about preparing for it. By identifying emerging trends and anticipating changes in the market, you can position your business to capitalize on new opportunities and mitigate potential risks. This may involve adjusting your product offerings, updating your marketing messaging, or exploring new distribution channels to stay ahead of the curve.

PRACTICAL GUIDANCE FOR SMALL BUSINESS OWNERS

Armed with a deeper understanding of market research and analysis, let's explore some practical guidance to help you navigate the waters of the market with confidence and clarity.

1. **Start with Clear Objectives**: Before diving into market research, clarify your objectives and define what you hope to achieve. Whether it's understanding your target audience, assessing market demand, or evaluating competitive threats, having clear goals will guide your research efforts and ensure you stay focused on what matters most.

2. **Use a Mix of Qualitative and Quantitative Methods**: Market research can take many forms, from surveys and focus groups to interviews and observational studies. By using a mix of qualitative and quantitative methods, you can gain a comprehensive understanding of the market landscape and triangulate your findings for greater accuracy and depth.

3. **Leverage Online Resources and Tools**: The internet is a treasure trove of market research resources, from industry reports and market data providers to online surveys and social media analytics tools. Take advantage of these resources to gather insights, track trends, and monitor consumer sentiment in real-time.

4. **Don't Forget about Your Existing Customers**: While it's important to focus on attracting new customers, don't overlook the value of your existing customer base. Conducting customer satisfaction surveys, gathering feedback, and analyzing purchase history can provide valuable insights into customer preferences and behaviors, helping you tailor your offerings and improve retention.

5. **Stay Agile and Iterative**: The market is constantly evolving, and your research efforts should be too. Adopt an agile and iterative approach to market research, continuously gathering feedback, testing hypotheses, and refining your strategies based on new information and insights. By staying nimble and responsive, you can adapt to changing market conditions and maintain a competitive edge.

6. **Embrace Digital Transformation**: In today's digital age, embracing technology is no longer a choice—it's a necessity for survival. Explore digital marketing avenues such as social media advertising, search engine optimization (SEO), and content marketing to expand your reach and engage with your target audience effectively. Invest in user-friendly website design and mobile optimization to ensure seamless browsing experiences for your customers. Leverage customer relationship management (CRM) tools to manage and nurture your customer relationships, providing personalized experiences that drive loyalty and retention.

7. **Cultivate Brand Advocacy**: Your most valuable marketing asset isn't your budget or your ad spend—it's your loyal customers. Cultivate brand advocacy by exceeding customer expectations at every touchpoint, delivering exceptional products, services, and support that inspire rave reviews and referrals. Encourage

satisfied customers to share their experiences on social media, review platforms, and word-of-mouth channels, amplifying your brand's reach and influence organically. Invest in building a community around your brand, fostering a sense of belonging and camaraderie that transforms customers into loyal advocates and ambassadors.

8. **Stay Agile in Execution**: In the fast-paced world of business, agility is the name of the game. Keep your finger on the pulse of market trends, consumer behavior, and competitive dynamics, remaining nimble and responsive to change. Whether it's adjusting your messaging in response to shifting consumer preferences or pivoting your channel strategy to capitalize on emerging opportunities, agility is your greatest asset in navigating the winds of change.

9. **Invest in Education and Development**: The world of marketing is vast and ever-evolving, with new technologies, trends, and strategies emerging at a rapid pace. Invest in your own education and development, staying informed about the latest industry insights, best practices, and innovations. Attend workshops, webinars, and conferences to expand your knowledge and network with industry peers. Enroll in online courses and certifications to deepen your expertise in areas such as digital marketing, analytics, and consumer behavior. By investing in continuous learning and professional development, you equip yourself with the skills and insights needed to stay ahead of the curve and drive meaningful results for your business.

10. **Foster a Culture of Innovation**: Innovation is the lifeblood of business growth, driving creativity, differentiation, and competitive advantage. Foster a culture of innovation within your organization, empowering employees at all levels to contribute ideas,

experiment with new approaches, and challenge the status quo. Create dedicated spaces and initiatives for brainstorming, ideation, and collaboration, providing resources and support for innovative projects to flourish. Celebrate and recognize successful innovations, whether they result in incremental improvements or transformative breakthroughs, fostering a culture of curiosity, risk-taking, and continuous improvement that fuels long-term success.

CONCLUSION

In this expanded chapter, we've delved deep into the waters of market research and analysis, uncovering its importance, exploring its intricacies, and providing practical guidance for small business owners to navigate the complexities of the market with confidence and clarity. By understanding the motivations behind consumer behavior, mapping out the competitive landscape, and forecasting trends, you can chart a course toward success in today's dynamic business environment. So set your compass, hoist your sails, and embark on this exciting journey with the knowledge that you're equipped to navigate the sea of customer insights with skill and determination.

CHAPTER 3
Setting Marketing Objectives: Plotting Your Course for Success

Ahoy, fellow captain of commerce! Welcome to the helm as we navigate the waters of setting marketing objectives—a crucial step in charting a course for your business's success. In this chapter, we'll unfurl the sails of strategy, delve into the depths of goal setting, and equip you with the navigational tools needed to steer your ship toward prosperous shores.

UNDERSTANDING THE IMPORTANCE OF MARKETING OBJECTIVES

Imagine your business as a ship setting sail on the vast ocean of opportunity. Without a destination in mind, you risk drifting aimlessly, at the mercy of unpredictable winds and currents. Marketing objectives serve as your guiding star, providing clarity of purpose and direction for your efforts.

At its essence, setting marketing objectives is about defining what you hope to achieve with your marketing endeavors. Whether it's increasing brand awareness, driving sales, or expanding your customer base, clear and measurable objectives provide a roadmap for success. They serve as a beacon of light on the horizon, guiding your decisions and actions toward tangible outcomes.

PLOTTING YOUR COURSE: THE SMART APPROACH TO GOAL SETTING

Now that we understand why marketing objectives are important, let's delve into the process of setting them. One popular framework for goal setting is the SMART approach—Specific, Measurable, Achievable, Relevant, and Time-bound.

- **Specific**: Your objectives should be clear and well-defined, leaving no room for ambiguity. Instead of vague statements like "increase sales," strive for specificity. For example, "increase online sales by 20% within the next six months" provides a clear target to aim for.

- **Measurable**: To gauge your progress and success, your objectives should be measurable. This means quantifying your goals in terms of metrics or key performance indicators (KPIs) that can be tracked over time. For instance, if your objective is to boost website traffic, you might measure it in terms of page views, unique visitors, or conversion rates.

- **Achievable**: While it's important to aim high, your objectives should also be realistic and attainable. Consider your resources, capabilities, and constraints when setting goals, and ensure they are within reach with the right strategy and effort. Setting overly ambitious goals can lead to frustration and demotivation if they're not achievable.

- **Relevant**: Your objectives should align with your overall business goals and mission. They should be relevant to your industry, target audience, and competitive landscape. For example, if your business is focused on sustainability, your marketing objectives might include initiatives to reduce environmental impact or promote eco-friendly products.

- **Time-bound**: Finally, your objectives should have a timeframe attached to them, providing a sense of urgency and accountability. Setting deadlines creates a sense of momentum and focus, driving you to take action and make progress toward your goals. Whether it's weeks, months, or quarters, establish clear timelines for achieving your objectives.

PRACTICAL GUIDANCE FOR SMALL BUSINESS OWNERS

Now that we've explored the SMART approach to goal setting, let's dive deeper into practical guidance for setting marketing objectives that propel your business forward.

1. **Start with Your Business Goals**: Before setting marketing objectives, it's essential to align them with your broader business goals and objectives. Consider what you hope to achieve as a company—whether it's increasing revenue, expanding market share, or launching new products—and ensure your marketing objectives support these overarching aims.

2. **Conduct a SWOT Analysis**: A SWOT analysis—examining your business's strengths, weaknesses, opportunities, and threats—can provide valuable insights that inform your marketing objectives. By understanding your internal capabilities and external market dynamics, you can identify areas for improvement and opportunities for growth that shape your objectives.

3. **Understand Your Target Audience**: Your marketing objectives should be informed by a deep understanding of your target audience—who they are, what they need, and how they make purchasing decisions. Conduct market research to gather insights into your audience's

demographics, psychographics, and behaviors, and tailor your objectives to address their needs and preferences effectively.

4. **Set Priorities and Focus Areas**: With limited resources and competing priorities, it's important to focus your efforts on a few key objectives that will have the greatest impact on your business. Identify the areas of opportunity that align with your strengths and market opportunities, and prioritize them based on their potential for growth and return on investment.

5. **Break Down Your Objectives**: Large, ambitious objectives can be daunting, so break them down into smaller, manageable tasks or milestones. This not only makes them more achievable but also provides a roadmap for progress and accountability. For example, if your objective is to increase social media engagement, you might break it down into specific actions such as posting frequency, content types, and engagement metrics to track.

6. **Track and Measure Progress**: Once you've set your objectives, establish a system for tracking and measuring your progress over time. Use relevant metrics and KPIs to monitor your performance against your goals, and adjust your strategy as needed based on the data. Regularly review your objectives and make course corrections as necessary to stay on track toward success.

CONCLUSION

In this chapter, we've navigated the waters of setting marketing objectives, understanding their importance, exploring the SMART approach to goal setting, and providing practical guidance for small business owners to chart their course for success. By aligning your objectives with your broader business goals, leveraging the SMART framework, and staying focused on priorities, you can steer your ship toward prosperous horizons with confidence and clarity. So, hoist your sails, set your sights on the horizon, and embark on this exciting journey with a clear sense of purpose and direction. Smooth sailing awaits!

CHAPTER 4
Crafting Your Unique Value Proposition: Setting Your Business Apart

Ahoy, fellow entrepreneurs! Welcome to the shores of crafting your unique value proposition—a beacon that distinguishes your business from the sea of competitors. In this chapter, we'll embark on a voyage into the heart of value creation, uncovering the essence of what makes your business truly unique and irresistible to your target audience.

UNDERSTANDING THE SIGNIFICANCE OF YOUR UNIQUE VALUE PROPOSITION

Imagine your business as a treasure chest waiting to be discovered by eager adventurers. Your unique value proposition is the key that unlocks the riches within, enticing customers to choose you over the competition. It's more than just a catchy slogan or a clever tagline—it's the promise you make to your customers, the reason they should do business with you instead of your competitors.

At its core, your unique value proposition is about answering the fundamental question: "Why should I choose you?" It's about articulating the unique blend of features, benefits, and experiences that set your business apart and create value for your customers. By clearly communicating your value proposition, you make it easier for customers to understand what makes you special and why they should choose you over alternatives.

CRAFTING YOUR UNIQUE VALUE PROPOSITION: THE ART AND SCIENCE OF DIFFERENTIATION

Crafting a compelling value proposition is both an art and a science, requiring creativity, insight, and strategic thinking. It's about understanding your target audience's needs and desires, identifying gaps in the market, and positioning your business in a way that resonates with your customers. Let's dive deeper into the elements that comprise a strong value proposition:

1. **Identify Your Unique Selling Points (USPs)**: What sets your business apart from the competition? Whether it's superior quality, innovative features, exceptional customer service, or unbeatable prices, your unique selling points are the foundation of your value proposition. Take stock of your strengths and capabilities, and identify the aspects of your business that provide the most value to your customers.

2. **Understand Your Customer's Pain Points and Desires**: To craft a value proposition that resonates with your audience, you need to understand their pain points, challenges, and aspirations. What problems are they trying to solve? What goals are they trying to

achieve? By empathizing with your customers and understanding their needs on a deeper level, you can tailor your value proposition to address their specific concerns and desires.

3. **Communicate the Benefits, Not Just the Features**: While it's important to highlight the features of your product or service, what truly resonates with customers are the benefits they derive from using it. Instead of focusing solely on what your product does, emphasize how it solves your customer's problems, improves their lives, or fulfills their desires. For example, a lawn care service might not just mow lawns but also save customers time, beautify their homes, and enhance their quality of life.

4. **Be Clear, Concise, and Compelling**: In a world inundated with marketing messages, clarity and simplicity are key. Your value proposition should be easy to understand, memorable, and impactful. Avoid jargon and technical language, and instead use plain language that resonates with your target audience. Consider using visuals, storytelling, or metaphors to bring your value proposition to life and make it more engaging.

5. **Show Proof and Social Validation**: To build trust and credibility, back up your value proposition with evidence and social proof. Whether it's customer testimonials, case studies, awards, or certifications, providing tangible proof of your claims helps alleviate customer skepticism and reinforces the value of choosing your business. Highlighting your track record of success and satisfied customers can help differentiate you from competitors and build confidence in your offerings.

PRACTICAL GUIDANCE FOR SMALL BUSINESS OWNERS

Now that we understand the elements of a strong value proposition, let's explore some practical guidance for crafting one that sets your business apart and resonates with your target audience:

1. **Conduct Market Research**: Start by conducting market research to gain insights into your target audience's needs, preferences, and pain points. Identify gaps in the market and opportunities for differentiation that align with your strengths and capabilities.

2. **Define Your Target Audience**: Clearly define your target audience and segment them based on demographic, psychographic, and behavioral factors. Understanding who you're trying to reach allows you to tailor your value proposition to their specific needs and preferences.

3. **Analyze Your Competitors**: Conduct a competitive analysis to understand how your competitors are positioning themselves in the market and what unique value propositions they're offering. Identify areas of opportunity where you can differentiate yourself and offer something truly unique and compelling.

4. **Identify Your Unique Selling Points**: Take stock of your business's strengths, capabilities, and USPs. What

sets you apart from the competition? Whether it's product features, service offerings, pricing, or customer experience, identify the aspects of your business that provide the most value to your customers.

5. **Craft Your Value Proposition**: Use the insights gathered from your research to craft a value proposition that resonates with your target audience and highlights your unique selling points. Keep it clear, concise, and compelling, and focus on communicating the benefits your customers will experience by choosing your business.

6. **Test and Iterate**: Once you've crafted your value proposition, test it with your target audience to gauge its effectiveness and gather feedback. Iterate and refine your value proposition based on the insights gained from testing, and continue to monitor its performance over time.

CONCLUSION

In this chapter, we've explored the importance of crafting a unique value proposition that sets your business apart from the competition and resonates with your target audience. By understanding your customer's needs and desires, identifying your unique selling points, and crafting a clear and compelling value proposition, you can differentiate your business and attract customers in a crowded marketplace. So, hoist your flag, stand tall, and let your unique value proposition be the guiding star that leads customers to your shores. Smooth sailing awaits!

CHAPTER 5
Selecting Marketing Channels: Navigating the Seas of Promotion

Ahoy, savvy entrepreneurs! Welcome to the captain's deck as we set sail into the vast ocean of marketing channels—a treasure trove of opportunities to promote your business and connect with your target audience. In this chapter, we'll hoist the sails, unfurl the flags, and navigate the waters of selecting the right marketing channels to steer your business toward success.

UNDERSTANDING THE SIGNIFICANCE OF MARKETING CHANNELS

Picture your business as a majestic ship sailing through uncharted waters. Marketing channels are the wind in your sails, propelling you forward and guiding you toward your destination. They are the pathways through which you communicate with your audience, raise awareness of your brand, and drive engagement and conversions.

At its core, selecting the right marketing channels is about reaching your target audience where they are most likely to be found. It's about casting your net in the right fishing grounds, ensuring that your message resonates with the right people at the right time and in the right place. By choosing the most effective channels for your business, you can maximize your reach, optimize your resources, and achieve your marketing objectives more efficiently.

NAVIGATING THE SEAS OF MARKETING CHANNELS: EXPLORING YOUR OPTIONS

The marketing landscape is vast and varied, with a myriad of channels and platforms to choose from. From traditional channels like print and television to digital channels like social media and email, the options can seem overwhelming. Let's explore some of the most common marketing channels and their respective strengths and weaknesses:

1. **Social Media Marketing**: Social media platforms like Facebook, Instagram, Twitter, and LinkedIn offer a powerful way to reach and engage with your target audience. With billions of users worldwide, social media provides unparalleled opportunities to build brand awareness, drive website traffic, and foster customer relationships. However, it requires careful planning and execution to cut through the noise and stand out amidst the competition.

2. **Content Marketing**: Content marketing involves creating and distributing valuable, relevant, and consistent content to attract and retain a clearly defined audience. This can include blog posts, articles, videos,

podcasts, infographics, and more. Content marketing helps establish your brand as a thought leader in your industry, build trust with your audience, and drive organic traffic to your website. However, it requires time, effort, and resources to produce high-quality content that resonates with your target audience.

3. **Email Marketing**: Email marketing remains one of the most effective channels for driving customer engagement and conversions. With email, you can deliver personalized messages directly to your audience's inbox, nurturing leads, promoting products and services, and driving repeat business. However, email marketing requires careful segmentation, targeting, and optimization to avoid being labeled as spam and to maximize open and click-through rates.

4. **Search Engine Optimization (SEO)**: SEO is the process of optimizing your website to rank higher in search engine results pages (SERPs) for relevant keywords and phrases. By improving your website's visibility and accessibility to search engines, you can attract more organic traffic and generate leads and sales. However, SEO is a long-term strategy that requires ongoing effort and patience to see results, and it's subject to algorithm changes and competition from other websites.

5. **Pay-Per-Click (PPC) Advertising**: PPC advertising allows you to bid on keywords and display ads on search engines like Google and social media platforms like Facebook and LinkedIn. You only pay when someone clicks on your ad, making it a cost-effective way to drive targeted traffic to your website and generate leads and sales. However, PPC can be competitive and expensive, and it requires careful keyword selection, ad targeting, and budget management to achieve a positive return on investment.

PRACTICAL GUIDANCE FOR SMALL BUSINESS OWNERS

Now that we've explored some of the most common marketing channels, let's dive into practical guidance for selecting the right channels for your business:

1. **Know Your Audience**: Start by understanding your target audience—who they are, what they need, and where they spend their time online. Conduct market research, gather demographic and psychographic data, and create customer personas to inform your channel selection.

2. **Set Clear Objectives**: Define your marketing objectives and goals, whether it's increasing brand awareness, driving website traffic, generating leads, or boosting sales. Your objectives will help guide your channel selection and measurement efforts.

3. **Consider Your Budget and Resources**: Evaluate your budget and resources to determine which marketing channels are feasible for your business. Some channels may require significant investment in terms of time, money, and manpower, while others may offer more cost-effective options.

4. **Evaluate Channel Effectiveness**: Assess the effectiveness of each marketing channel based on factors like reach, engagement, conversion rates, and

return on investment. Look at past performance data, case studies, and industry benchmarks to inform your decision-making process.

5. **Test and Iterate**: Don't be afraid to experiment with different marketing channels and strategies to see what works best for your business. Start small, test different approaches, and gather data and feedback to inform your decisions. Continuously monitor and optimize your efforts based on performance metrics and customer feedback.

6. **Integrate Your Channels**: Consider how different marketing channels can work together to create a cohesive and integrated marketing strategy. For example, you can use social media to promote your content, email marketing to nurture leads, and PPC advertising to drive targeted traffic to your website. By integrating your channels, you can maximize their impact and effectiveness.

CONCLUSION

In this chapter, we've navigated the seas of marketing channels, exploring the options available to small business owners and providing practical guidance for selecting the right channels for your business. By understanding your audience, setting clear objectives, evaluating channel effectiveness, and testing and iterating on your efforts, you can navigate the waters of promotion with confidence and clarity. So, hoist your flags, set your course, and embark on this exciting journey knowing that you have the knowledge and tools to navigate the seas of marketing channels with skill and determination. Smooth sailing awaits!

CHAPTER 6
Developing Your Marketing Mix: Blending Strategies for Success

Ahoy, fellow entrepreneurs! Welcome aboard as we embark on a voyage into the heart of developing your marketing mix—a brew of strategies and tactics that will propel your business to new heights. In this chapter, we'll set our sights on the horizon, explore the elements of the marketing mix, and equip you with the knowledge and tools to craft a winning formula for success.

UNDERSTANDING THE MARKETING MIX: A RECIPE FOR SUCCESS

Imagine your business as a master chef preparing a feast for hungry diners. Your marketing mix is the recipe that guides your culinary creations, combining the right ingredients in the right proportions to satisfy your customers' appetites. It's more than just a list of tactics—it's a strategic framework that aligns your product, price, place, and promotion to meet the needs and preferences of your target audience.

At its essence, the marketing mix consists of four key elements:

1. **Product**: This refers to the goods or services you offer to your customers. It encompasses everything from product features and design to packaging and branding. Your product is the foundation of your marketing mix, and its quality, features, and benefits play a crucial role in shaping your customers' perceptions and experiences.

2. **Price**: Price is the amount of money customers are willing to pay for your product or service. It's influenced by factors such as production costs, competitor pricing, and perceived value. Setting the right price is essential for balancing profitability with affordability and ensuring that your offering remains competitive in the market.

3. **Place**: Place refers to the distribution channels through which your product or service is made available to customers. It includes physical locations such as retail stores, as well as online channels such as e-commerce websites and marketplaces. Choosing the right distribution channels ensures that your product reaches your target audience efficiently and effectively.

4. **Promotion**: Promotion encompasses the various tactics and strategies you use to communicate with your target audience and persuade them to buy your product or service. This includes advertising, public relations, sales promotions, direct marketing, and more. Effective promotion helps raise awareness of your brand, generate interest in your offering, and ultimately drive sales and revenue.

CRAFTING YOUR MARKETING MIX: BLENDING STRATEGIES FOR SUCCESS

Now that we understand the elements of the marketing mix, let's explore how to craft a winning formula for your business:

1. **Product Strategy**: Start by defining your product strategy, including the features, benefits, and positioning of your offering. Consider factors such as product design, packaging, branding, and customer experience. What sets your product apart from the competition, and how can you communicate its unique value to your target audience?

2. **Pricing Strategy**: Next, develop a pricing strategy that reflects the value of your product or service while remaining competitive in the market. Consider factors such as production costs, competitor pricing, and customer willingness to pay. Are you positioning your offering as a premium product, a budget-friendly option, or something in between?

3. **Distribution Strategy**: Determine the most effective

distribution channels for reaching your target audience and delivering your product or service to them. Consider factors such as geographic reach, customer preferences, and channel availability. Are you selling through physical retail stores, online marketplaces, or a combination of both?

4. **Promotional Strategy**: Develop a promotional strategy that effectively communicates your message and persuades customers to buy. Consider your target audience, their media consumption habits, and the most effective channels for reaching them. Are you using advertising, social media, content marketing, or a mix of tactics to raise awareness and drive engagement?

PRACTICAL GUIDANCE FOR SMALL BUSINESS OWNERS

Now that we've explored the elements of the marketing mix, let's dive into some practical guidance for developing your own mix:

1. **Know Your Audience**: Start by understanding your target audience—who they are, what they need, and how they make purchasing decisions. Conduct market research, gather demographic and psychographic data, and create customer personas to inform your marketing mix decisions.

2. **Align with Business Goals**: Ensure that your marketing mix aligns with your broader business goals and objectives. Consider what you hope to achieve—whether it's increasing sales, expanding market share, or launching new products—and tailor your mix accordingly.

3. **Test and Iterate**: Don't be afraid to experiment with different strategies and tactics to see what works best for your business. Start small, test different approaches, and gather data and feedback to inform your decisions. Continuously monitor and optimize your mix based on performance metrics and customer feedback.

4. **Integrate Your Mix**: Consider how different elements of your marketing mix can work together to create a

cohesive and integrated strategy. For example, you can use content marketing to raise awareness, social media to engage with your audience, and email marketing to nurture leads and drive conversions. By integrating your mix, you can maximize its impact and effectiveness.

5. **Stay Agile and Responsive**: The marketing landscape is constantly evolving, so it's essential to stay agile and responsive to changes in the market. Keep abreast of industry trends, consumer preferences, and competitive dynamics, and be prepared to adjust your marketing mix accordingly. Whether it's shifting consumer behavior, emerging technologies, or new competitors entering the market, agility is key to staying ahead of the curve.

CONCLUSION

In this chapter, we've explored the elements of the marketing mix and provided practical guidance for crafting a winning formula for your business. By understanding your product, pricing, distribution, and promotion strategies, you can develop a cohesive and effective marketing mix that drives success and growth. So, hoist your flags, set your course, and embark on this exciting journey knowing that you have the knowledge and tools to navigate the seas of marketing with skill and determination. Smooth sailing awaits!

CHAPTER 7
Creating a Marketing Plan: Charting Your Course for Success

Ahoy, fellow captains of commerce! Welcome to the helm as we set sail into the realm of creating a marketing plan—a crucial compass that guides your business toward its goals. In this chapter, we'll unfurl the maps, plot the coordinates, and equip you with the tools and strategies needed to navigate the seas of marketing with confidence and clarity.

UNDERSTANDING THE IMPORTANCE OF A MARKETING PLAN

Imagine your business as a ship embarking on a grand voyage. Without a map to guide your journey, you risk drifting aimlessly, at the mercy of unpredictable winds and currents. A marketing plan serves as your navigational chart, providing direction and clarity as you navigate the waters of promotion and engagement.

At its core, a marketing plan is a strategic roadmap that outlines your marketing objectives, strategies, and tactics for achieving your business goals. It's a blueprint that helps you identify your target audience, understand their needs and preferences, and determine the most effective ways to reach and engage with them. By creating a marketing plan, you set yourself up for success by aligning your efforts with your broader business objectives and ensuring that your resources are used efficiently and effectively.

CRAFTING YOUR MARKETING PLAN: A STEP-BY-STEP GUIDE

Now that we understand the importance of a marketing plan, let's dive into the process of crafting one for your business:

1. **Define Your Objectives**: Start by defining your marketing objectives—what you hope to achieve with your marketing efforts. Whether it's increasing brand awareness, driving sales, or expanding your customer base, your objectives should be specific, measurable, achievable, relevant, and time-bound (SMART).

2. **Know Your Audience**: Next, identify your target audience—who they are, what they need, and how they make purchasing decisions. Conduct market research, gather demographic and psychographic data, and create customer personas to inform your marketing strategy.

3. **Conduct a SWOT Analysis**: Conduct a SWOT analysis to identify your business's strengths, weaknesses, opportunities, and threats. This will help you understand your competitive position in the market, uncover areas for improvement, and identify opportunities for growth.

4. **Develop Your Strategies and Tactics**: Based on your objectives, audience research, and SWOT analysis, develop your marketing strategies and tactics. This may include a mix of promotional activities such

as advertising, content marketing, social media, email marketing, and more.

5. **Set Your Budget**: Determine your marketing budget based on your objectives, strategies, and available resources. Consider factors such as advertising costs, marketing software and tools, and personnel expenses. Allocate your budget strategically to ensure that you're maximizing your return on investment.

6. **Create a Timeline**: Develop a timeline or schedule for implementing your marketing plan. Break down your activities into manageable tasks and set deadlines for completion. This will help you stay organized, track your progress, and ensure that you're meeting your objectives on time.

7. **Measure and Evaluate**: Finally, establish key performance indicators (KPIs) to measure the success of your marketing efforts. Track metrics such as website traffic, social media engagement, lead generation, and sales conversions to gauge the effectiveness of your strategies and tactics. Regularly evaluate your performance and adjust your plan as needed to optimize your results.

PRACTICAL GUIDANCE FOR SMALL BUSINESS OWNERS

Now that we've outlined the steps for creating a marketing plan, let's dive into some practical guidance for small business owners:

1. **Keep It Simple and Flexible**: Your marketing plan doesn't need to be overly complicated or rigid. Keep it simple, focusing on the key objectives, strategies, and tactics that will drive results for your business. Be flexible and open to adjustments as you gather feedback and insights from your marketing activities.

2. **Focus on Your Unique Value Proposition**: Ensure that your marketing plan is aligned with your unique value proposition and positioning in the market. Highlight what sets your business apart from the competition and how you're addressing the needs and preferences of your target audience.

3. **Integrate Your Efforts**: Consider how different marketing channels and tactics can work together to create a cohesive and integrated marketing strategy. For example, you can use content marketing to raise awareness, social media to engage with your audience, and email marketing to nurture leads and drive conversions. By integrating your efforts, you can maximize their impact and effectiveness.

4. **Stay Updated on Trends and Insights**: The marketing landscape is constantly evolving, so it's essential to stay updated on industry trends, consumer behavior, and emerging technologies. Keep abreast of new developments in your industry, monitor your competitors, and adapt your marketing plan accordingly to stay ahead of the curve.

5. **Seek Feedback and Iterate**: Don't be afraid to seek feedback from customers, colleagues, and mentors on your marketing plan. Their insights and perspectives can provide valuable guidance and help you identify areas for improvement. Continuously iterate and refine your plan based on feedback and performance data to optimize your results.

CONCLUSION

In this chapter, we've explored the importance of creating a marketing plan and provided a step-by-step guide for crafting one for your business. By defining your objectives, knowing your audience, developing your strategies and tactics, setting your budget, creating a timeline, and measuring your results, you can navigate the seas of marketing with confidence and clarity. So, hoist your flags, set your course, and embark on this exciting journey knowing that you have the knowledge and tools to chart your course for success. Smooth sailing awaits!

CHAPTER 8
Implementing and Evaluating Your Marketing Strategy: Turning Plans into Action and Results

Ahoy, fellow entrepreneurs! Welcome to the final leg of our marketing voyage, where we dive into the exciting realm of implementing and evaluating your marketing strategy. In this chapter, we'll hoist the anchor, set sail, and guide you through the process of bringing your marketing plans to life, measuring their effectiveness, and steering your business toward success.

UNDERSTANDING THE IMPORTANCE OF IMPLEMENTATION AND EVALUATION

Imagine your business as a ship setting sail on a grand expedition. Without skilled sailors to man the decks and navigate the waters, your journey would be doomed to drift aimlessly. Similarly, implementing and evaluating your marketing strategy is the crew that breathes life into your plans, ensures they stay on course, and guides you toward your destination.

Implementation is the process of putting your marketing plans into action—executing the strategies and tactics outlined in your marketing plan. It involves coordinating resources, managing timelines, and overseeing the day-to-day execution of your marketing activities. Evaluation, on the other hand, is the process of assessing the effectiveness of your marketing efforts, measuring their impact on your business goals, and identifying areas for improvement.

By implementing and evaluating your marketing strategy effectively, you can ensure that your efforts are aligned with your business objectives, optimize your resources, and maximize your return on investment.

IMPLEMENTING YOUR MARKETING STRATEGY: PUTTING PLANS INTO ACTION

Now that we understand the importance of implementation, let's dive into the process of bringing your marketing plans to life:

1. **Allocate Resources**: Start by allocating the necessary resources—such as budget, personnel, and tools—to support your marketing efforts. Ensure that you have the infrastructure and support in place to execute your plans effectively.

2. **Assign Responsibilities**: Clearly define roles and responsibilities for each member of your team involved in implementing the marketing strategy. Establish clear lines of communication and accountability to ensure that everyone is on the same page and working toward common goals.

3. **Create a Timeline**: Develop a timeline or schedule for implementing your marketing activities. Break down your plans into actionable tasks, set deadlines for completion, and establish milestones to track progress.

4. **Execute Your Plans**: With your resources allocated, responsibilities assigned, and timeline in place, it's time

to put your plans into action. Execute your marketing activities according to the schedule, monitoring progress and addressing any issues or challenges that arise along the way.

5. **Adapt and Iterate**: Be prepared to adapt and iterate on your plans as needed based on feedback and insights gathered during the implementation process. Stay agile and responsive to changes in the market, consumer behavior, and competitive dynamics, adjusting your strategy as necessary to stay on course toward your goals.

EVALUATING YOUR MARKETING STRATEGY: MEASURING IMPACT AND EFFECTIVENESS

Once your marketing activities are underway, it's essential to evaluate their impact and effectiveness. Here's how you can assess the success of your efforts:

1. **Set Key Performance Indicators (KPIs)**: Establish KPIs to measure the success of your marketing activities. These may include metrics such as website traffic, social media engagement, lead generation, conversion rates, customer acquisition costs, and return on investment.

2. **Gather Data and Insights**: Use tools and analytics platforms to gather data and insights on the performance of your marketing campaigns. Monitor KPIs regularly, track progress over time, and identify trends and patterns that may indicate areas of success or areas for improvement.

3. **Compare Results to Objectives**: Compare your results to the objectives outlined in your marketing plan. Are you meeting your targets for brand awareness, lead generation, sales, or other key goals? Identify any gaps

or discrepancies and investigate the reasons behind them.

4. **Seek Feedback from Stakeholders**: Gather feedback from customers, colleagues, and other stakeholders on their perceptions of your marketing efforts. What is working well, and what could be improved? Use this feedback to inform your evaluation and identify areas for optimization.

5. **Iterate and Improve**: Based on your evaluation findings, make adjustments to your marketing strategy to optimize performance and drive better results. Continuously iterate and improve your tactics, experimenting with new approaches and tactics to see what works best for your business.

PRACTICAL GUIDANCE FOR SMALL BUSINESS OWNERS

Now that we've covered the fundamentals of implementing and evaluating your marketing strategy, let's explore some practical guidance for small business owners:

1. **Stay Focused on Goals**: Keep your business objectives front and center throughout the implementation and evaluation process. Ensure that your marketing activities are aligned with your broader goals and are driving measurable results that contribute to your success.

2. **Monitor Progress Regularly**: Stay proactive in monitoring the progress of your marketing efforts. Regularly review your KPIs, track performance against targets, and identify any areas of concern or opportunity that require attention.

3. **Be Open to Feedback**: Be open to feedback from customers, colleagues, and other stakeholders on the effectiveness of your marketing activities. Listen attentively to their insights and perspectives, and use them to inform your evaluation and decision-making process.

4. **Celebrate Successes**: Take the time to celebrate successes and milestones achieved along the way. Recognize and reward your team for their hard work and

dedication, and use positive reinforcement to motivate continued excellence in execution.

5. **Stay Agile and Adaptive**: In today's fast-paced business environment, agility and adaptability are key to success. Be prepared to pivot and adjust your marketing strategy in response to changing market conditions, emerging trends, and new opportunities that arise.

CONCLUSION

In this final chapter, we've explored the critical importance of implementing and evaluating your marketing strategy and provided practical guidance for small business owners to navigate this process effectively. By putting your plans into action, measuring their impact, and continuously iterating and improving based on feedback and insights, you can steer your business toward success with confidence and clarity. So, hoist your flags, set your course, and embark on this exciting journey knowing that you have the knowledge and tools to navigate the seas of marketing with skill and determination. Smooth sailing awaits!

CHAPTER 9
Adapting and Refining Your Strategy: Navigating the Winds of Change

Ahoy, resilient entrepreneurs! Welcome to the ever-changing seas of business strategy, where agility and adaptability are the compasses that guide us through turbulent waters. In this chapter, we'll explore the art of adapting and refining your marketing strategy—a crucial skill for small business owners navigating the unpredictable currents of the marketplace.

UNDERSTANDING THE NEED FOR ADAPTATION

Picture your business as a sturdy ship sailing through dynamic waters. Just as the winds and currents of the sea are ever-shifting, so too are the forces shaping the business landscape. In today's fast-paced world, standing still is not an option. To thrive amidst change, small business owners must embrace adaptability as a cornerstone of their strategy.

Adaptation involves recognizing shifts in the market, customer preferences, technology, and competitive dynamics, and adjusting your strategy accordingly. It's about staying nimble, responsive, and proactive in the face of uncertainty, seizing opportunities, and mitigating risks as they arise.

THE ART OF ADAPTING YOUR STRATEGY

Now, let's delve into the art of adapting and refining your marketing strategy:

1. **Stay Informed**: Keep your finger on the pulse of the market by staying informed about industry trends, consumer behavior, and competitive developments. Regularly monitor news, market research reports, and industry publications to identify emerging opportunities and threats.

2. **Listen to Your Customers**: Your customers are your compass in navigating the seas of business. Listen attentively to their feedback, suggestions, and complaints, and use them as valuable insights into their needs, preferences, and pain points. Conduct surveys, interviews, and focus groups to gather feedback directly from your target audience.

3. **Monitor Performance Metrics**: Keep a close eye on key performance indicators (KPIs) to gauge the effectiveness of your marketing efforts. Track metrics such as website traffic, conversion rates, customer acquisition costs, and return on investment to measure the impact of your strategies and tactics.

4. **Be Flexible and Agile**: Flexibility and agility are essential qualities for navigating the uncertainties of the business world. Be prepared to pivot and adjust your strategy in response to changing circumstances,

emerging trends, and new opportunities. Embrace experimentation and iteration as tools for continuous improvement.

5. **Embrace Innovation**: Innovation is the wind in your sails, propelling your business forward into uncharted waters. Don't be afraid to think outside the box, explore new ideas, and experiment with innovative approaches to marketing and business development. Embrace technology as a catalyst for innovation, leveraging digital tools and platforms to reach and engage with your audience in new ways.

PRACTICAL GUIDANCE FOR SMALL BUSINESS OWNERS

Now, let's explore some practical guidance for small business owners looking to adapt and refine their marketing strategy:

1. **Conduct Regular Strategy Reviews**: Schedule regular strategy reviews to assess the effectiveness of your marketing efforts and identify areas for improvement. Set aside time each quarter or year to evaluate your performance, gather feedback, and make adjustments to your strategy as needed.

2. **Stay Agile and Responsive**: Agility is the name of the game in today's fast-paced business environment. Be prepared to pivot and adapt your strategy in response to changes in the market, shifts in consumer behavior, and new competitive threats. Stay nimble, responsive, and proactive in addressing emerging challenges and opportunities.

3. **Invest in Continuous Learning**: Keep investing in your own growth and development as a business owner and marketer. Stay curious, open-minded, and eager to learn new skills, tools, and techniques that can help you adapt and thrive in a changing landscape. Attend industry conferences, workshops, and webinars, and seek out opportunities for professional development

and networking.

4. **Build a Culture of Innovation**: Foster a culture of innovation within your organization, where creativity, experimentation, and risk-taking are encouraged and rewarded. Create a safe space for employees to share ideas, collaborate on projects, and explore new opportunities for growth and innovation. Celebrate successes and learn from failures as valuable lessons in the journey of adaptation.

5. **Stay True to Your Core Values**: While adaptation is essential for survival in a dynamic marketplace, it's also important to stay true to your core values and principles as a business. Maintain a clear sense of purpose and identity, and ensure that your adaptations align with your broader mission, vision, and values. This will help you stay grounded and focused amidst the whirlwind of change.

CONCLUSION

In this chapter, we've explored the art of adapting and refining your marketing strategy—a crucial skill for small business owners navigating the unpredictable currents of the marketplace. By staying informed, listening to your customers, monitoring performance metrics, embracing flexibility and agility, and fostering a culture of innovation, you can navigate the winds of change with confidence and resilience. So, hoist your flags, set your course, and embrace the journey of adaptation knowing that you have the knowledge and tools to navigate the seas of business with skill and determination. Smooth sailing awaits!

CHAPTER 10
Case Studies and Best Practices: Learning from the Successes of Others

Ahoy, fellow entrepreneurs! Welcome to the treasure trove of wisdom and insights found in the world of case studies and best practices. In this chapter, we'll embark on a journey through real-life stories of small businesses that have navigated the challenges of the marketplace and emerged victorious. By studying their successes and learning from their strategies, we'll uncover valuable lessons and practical guidance to inspire and guide your entrepreneurial endeavors.

THE POWER OF CASE STUDIES AND BEST PRACTICES

Imagine setting sail on a new venture, armed with nothing but a map and a compass. While charts and navigational tools are essential, there's no substitute for the wisdom gained from those who have sailed these waters before you. Case studies and best practices serve as beacons of light, illuminating the path to success and guiding you through the twists and turns of the entrepreneurial journey.

Case studies provide real-world examples of businesses facing specific challenges and achieving remarkable results. By examining their strategies, tactics, and outcomes, we can gain valuable insights into what works and what doesn't in the realm of business and marketing. Best practices, on the other hand, distill the collective wisdom of industry experts and thought leaders into actionable guidelines and principles for success.

UNCOVERING LESSONS FROM REAL-LIFE STORIES

Now, let's dive into the rich tapestry of case studies and best practices to uncover valuable lessons and practical guidance for small business owners:

1. Case Study: The Rise of a Local Bakery

Imagine a small bakery nestled in a bustling neighborhood, facing stiff competition from larger chain stores and online delivery services. Through a combination of quality products, personalized customer service, and creative marketing strategies, this bakery not only survived but thrived in a competitive market.

Key Takeaways:

- **Focus on Quality**: The bakery prioritized quality ingredients and craftsmanship, ensuring that every product was fresh, delicious, and made with care. This commitment to quality set them apart from their competitors and earned them a loyal customer base.

- **Build Relationships**: By getting to know their customers personally and building strong relationships within the community, the bakery fostered loyalty and repeat business. They hosted events, participated in local festivals, and engaged with customers on social media to create a sense of community around their brand.

- **Get Creative with Marketing**: From hosting baking classes to partnering with local events and charities, the bakery found innovative ways to promote their brand and attract new customers. They leveraged social media platforms like Instagram and Facebook to showcase their products and engage with their audience.

BEST PRACTICE: PERSONALIZED CUSTOMER EXPERIENCE

- **Know Your Customers**: Take the time to understand your customers' preferences, needs, and pain points. Tailor your products, services, and marketing efforts to meet their specific needs and preferences. Use tools like customer surveys, feedback forms, and social media listening to gather insights into what matters most to your audience.

- **Build Trust and Loyalty**: Foster trust and loyalty by providing exceptional customer service, going above and beyond to exceed expectations, and building genuine relationships with your customers. Be responsive to their needs and concerns, and show them that you value their business.

- **Stay Relevant and Innovative**: Keep your brand fresh and exciting by staying ahead of trends, experimenting with new ideas, and finding creative ways to engage with your audience. Monitor industry trends, keep an eye on what your competitors are doing, and be open to trying new strategies and tactics to stay relevant in a competitive market.

2. Case Study: The Success of an E-Commerce Startup

In the competitive world of e-commerce, standing out from the crowd can be a daunting challenge. Yet, one startup managed to carve out a niche for itself by focusing on a specific target audience and delivering a seamless shopping experience.

Key Takeaways:

- **Niche Targeting**: The startup identified a specific niche market with unique needs and preferences and tailored their products and marketing efforts accordingly. By focusing on a specific niche, they were able to differentiate themselves from larger competitors and attract a dedicated customer base.

- **User-Friendly Website**: By investing in a user-friendly website with intuitive navigation, high-quality images, and detailed product descriptions, the startup made it easy for customers to find and purchase products. They optimized their website for mobile devices and invested in fast, reliable hosting to ensure a seamless shopping experience.

- **Effective Digital Marketing**: Leveraging social media, email marketing, and influencer partnerships, the startup effectively reached and engaged with their target audience, driving traffic and sales to their website. They used targeted advertising campaigns on platforms like Facebook and Instagram to reach potential customers and retargeted website visitors with personalized offers and promotions.

BEST PRACTICE: NICHE TARGETING AND USER EXPERIENCE

- **Identify Your Niche**: Instead of trying to appeal to everyone, focus on a specific niche market with distinct needs and preferences. Conduct market research to identify underserved or overlooked segments of the market, and tailor your products, services, and marketing efforts to meet their needs.

- **Invest in User Experience**: Invest in creating a user-friendly website and online shopping experience that makes it easy for customers to find what they're looking for and complete their purchase. Pay attention to design, navigation, and functionality to ensure a seamless user experience across devices and platforms.

- **Maximize Your Digital Presence**: Leverage digital marketing channels such as social media, email marketing, and influencer partnerships to reach and engage with your target audience effectively. Experiment with different tactics and strategies to find what works best for your business, and invest in creating high-quality content and compelling visuals to capture attention and drive engagement.

PRACTICAL GUIDANCE FOR SMALL BUSINESS OWNERS

Now, let's distill the lessons from these case studies and best practices into practical guidance for small business owners:

1. **Know Your Audience**: Take the time to understand your target audience's preferences, needs, and behaviors. Conduct market research, gather feedback from customers, and analyze data to identify key trends and opportunities.

2. **Focus on Quality**: Prioritize quality in everything you do, from the products you offer to the customer service you provide. Delivering a consistently high-quality experience will foster trust, loyalty, and repeat business.

3. **Build Relationships**: Invest in building genuine relationships with your customers and community. Engage with them on a personal level, listen to their feedback, and show them that you value their business.

4. **Stay Innovative**: Don't be afraid to think outside the box and experiment with new ideas. Stay ahead of trends, embrace innovation, and find creative ways to differentiate your brand and offerings from the competition.

5. **Maximize Your Digital Presence**: Leverage digital marketing channels to reach and engage with your

target audience effectively. Experiment with different tactics and strategies to find what works best for your business, and invest in creating a seamless online shopping experience for your customers.

CONCLUSION

In this chapter, we've explored the power of case studies and best practices as valuable sources of wisdom and guidance for small business owners. By studying real-life examples of successful businesses and distilling their strategies and principles into actionable insights, we can gain valuable lessons and practical guidance to apply to our entrepreneurial endeavors. So, hoist your flags, set your course, and embark on this journey of learning and growth, knowing that you have the knowledge and tools to navigate the seas of business with skill and determination. Smooth sailing awaits!

CHAPTER 11
Conclusion: Anchoring Your Business Success

Ahoy, fellow captains of commerce! As we near the end of our voyage through the turbulent waters of business strategy and marketing, it's time to reflect on the lessons learned, the challenges overcome, and the victories achieved. In this final chapter, we'll weigh anchor and chart our course toward future success, armed with the knowledge and insights gained from our journey together.

REFLECTING ON THE JOURNEY

As small business owners, we know that the entrepreneurial journey is not for the faint of heart. It's a voyage filled with highs and lows, challenges and opportunities, setbacks and triumphs. Along the way, we've encountered fierce competition, shifting market dynamics, and unexpected obstacles. Yet, through determination, resilience, and a willingness to learn and adapt, we've navigated these challenges and steered our businesses toward success.

Throughout this guide, we've explored the fundamental principles of business strategy and marketing, from defining your vision and mission to crafting a compelling value proposition, identifying your target audience, and implementing effective marketing tactics. We've delved into the nuances of market research, setting objectives, selecting channels, developing a marketing mix, and creating a comprehensive marketing plan. We've learned from real-life case studies and best practices, gaining valuable insights into what it takes to succeed in today's competitive marketplace.

KEY TAKEAWAYS AND LESSONS LEARNED

As we conclude our journey, let's recap some of the key takeaways and lessons learned:

1. **Know Your Why**: At the heart of every successful business is a clear sense of purpose and mission. Define your why—the reason behind your business's existence—and let it guide every decision you make.

2. **Understand Your Audience**: Your customers are the compass that guides your business. Take the time to understand their needs, preferences, and pain points, and tailor your products, services, and marketing efforts to meet their specific needs.

3. **Differentiate Your Brand**: In a crowded marketplace, differentiation is key to standing out from the competition. Identify what sets your brand apart—whether it's quality, innovation, customer service, or something else—and leverage it to your advantage.

4. **Be Agile and Adaptive**: The business landscape is constantly evolving, so it's essential to stay agile and adaptive. Be willing to pivot and adjust your strategy in response to changing market conditions, emerging trends, and new opportunities.

5. **Invest in Relationships**: Building strong relationships with your customers, employees, suppliers, and other stakeholders is essential for long-term success. Foster trust, loyalty, and mutual respect, and prioritize the

well-being of those you do business with.

LOOKING TO THE FUTURE

As we bid farewell to the challenges of the past and set our sights on the horizon, it's important to remember that the journey is far from over. The seas of business are ever-changing, and new challenges and opportunities await us on the horizon. Yet, armed with the knowledge, insights, and experiences gained from our journey together, we are better equipped than ever to navigate the waters ahead.

As you continue on your entrepreneurial journey, remember to stay true to your vision, embrace change as an opportunity for growth, and never stop learning and adapting. Surround yourself with a supportive crew who shares your passion and dedication, and together, there's no limit to what you can achieve.

FINAL WORDS OF ENCOURAGEMENT

As we bring our voyage to a close, I'd like to offer a few final words of encouragement to my fellow entrepreneurs:

- **Believe in Yourself**: You have the passion, drive, and determination to succeed. Trust in your abilities, stay true to your vision, and never lose sight of your dreams.

- **Stay Resilient**: The road to success is rarely smooth, but every setback is an opportunity to learn and grow. Stay resilient in the face of adversity, and never let temporary defeats deter you from pursuing your goals.

- **Celebrate Your Successes**: Along the way, take the time to celebrate your successes, no matter how small. Acknowledge your achievements, recognize the hard work and dedication that went into them, and use them as fuel to propel you forward.

- **Keep Dreaming Big**: As you reach new milestones and achieve new levels of success, never stop dreaming big. The sky's the limit for what you can achieve, and with determination, perseverance, and a little bit of luck, you can turn your wildest dreams into reality.

In closing, I'd like to express my gratitude to every one of you for joining me on this journey. Whether you're a seasoned entrepreneur or just starting out on your business adventure, I hope that the insights and guidance shared in this guide have inspired and empowered you to chart your course toward success. Remember, the greatest adventures often begin with a single step. So, hoist your flags, set your course, and may the winds of fortune be ever in your favor. Fair winds and following seas, my friends!

www.ingramcontent.com/pod-product-compliance
Lightning Source LLC
Chambersburg PA
CBHW050119230526
45470CB00004B/1898